Defiant Joy

What Happens When You're Full of It

STUDY GUIDE

SIX SESSIONS

BY CANDACE PAYNE

WITH KEVIN AND SHERRY HARNEY

HarperChristian Resources

Defiant Joy Study Guide
© 2017 by Candace Payne

Requests for information should be addressed to:
HarperChristian Resources, 3900 Sparks Dr. SE, Grand Rapids, Michigan 49546

ISBN 978-0-310-09053-3 (softcover)
ISBN 978-0-310-09054-0 (ebook)

HarperChristian Resources titles may be purchased in bulk for church, business, fundraising, or ministry use. For information, please e-mail ResourceSpecialist@ChurchSource.com.

Cover design and all illustrations: Candace Payne
Interior design: Kait Lamphere
Interior imagery: istock.com/ThomasVogel

First Printing September 2017 / Printed in the United States of America

23 24 25 26 27 LBC 7 6 5 4 3

Defiant Joy

ALSO BY CANDACE PAYNE

Laugh It Up! (book, ebook, and audio book)

CONTENTS

A WORD FROM CANDACE

Hey there, Friend!

    I couldn't be more humbled and honored that you are here in these pages with me. Listen. I know how intimidating a study guide can be. It automatically sounds like a bore because it has the word *study* in it. But I know that if you're anything like me, you are longing for something more. You're longing to feel more deeply and get outside the box you're living inside.

    So, you bought a book from the lady who had a viral video entertaining herself with a child's toy? I get it. Out of all the studies to jump into, this one felt safe. And you're right. I hope joy is found for those who are professional study guide fill-in-the-blankers *and* for those who've never even imagined themselves opening a study guide unless they needed to pass an exam. The truth is you are me and I am you. And together we come to this guide with different life experiences and lenses that have left us wondering if there's more to this life.

    I pray you'll find there is most certainly more to the routine and mundane life you may have witnessed in days past or currently feel buried underneath. I pray you'll find the courage to fully engage in each assignment, answer with brutal authenticity every question, and discover what it means to live daily with defiant joy.

Sincerely,

INTRODUCTION:
JOY IS CLOSER THAN YOU THINK

That sounds so pretty, doesn't it? Joy is closer than you think. *Awwww. That's so special, Candace.* Y'all. I am sick and tired of mantras as much as the next person. I am. But I couldn't think of a better way to convey what you most need to believe before you jump into this study. Joy is most certainly near. There's a foundational truth that I will be building every thought about joy upon: God is good and He always does good. Because of this, He is the giver of every good and perfect gift. He has designed you to live a life that is full and abundant.

I have had people write to me and tell me that joy is a frivolous luxury. And, ultimately, that is telling me that they believe God is cruel and unkind and makes us work and perform and be deserving of anything good . . . especially joy. That's simply not the God I know or see throughout the Bible. Because God is good and always does good, I can trust that His promise to give me abundant life will include good things. What's more "good" than the nearness of our heavenly Father and the fullness of His joy right there by His side? Joy is closer than you think because God is better than you may believe.

Did ya catch that? I mean, REALLY catch that last statement?

Joy is closer than you think because God
is better than you may believe.

If you'll keep that as the filter for everything you will read after this, I know you'll be surprised at the measure of joy you can and will find.

Who's in?

Alrighty, then.

Here we go.

Session One

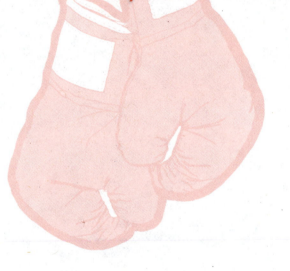

LAUGH IT UP, LIVE IT OUT

WHEN GOD SHOWS UP AND THINGS BLOW UP . . . IN A GOOD WAY!

My life changed when I put on a Chewbacca mask, cracked up at myself, and over 160 million people laughed along with me. I still have not figured out exactly what was going on that day in my van. I don't fully understand what happened the next few days when I was invited to appear on TV shows and interviewed by people I had only seen on a screen up to that point in my life. But here are a few things I am learning through this experience.

We were made for laughter, joy, and fun . . . more than we realize. Our hearts and souls long for joy. I believe there is a God who delights when we laugh and celebrates when we play.

God has a destiny for each of us. It is better than we dream. And He will move us toward our destiny in surprising and shocking ways. God might not use a *Star Wars* mask and the internet to unfold your destiny, but He has a plan and it is going to be a fun ride, if you are willing to jump on.

To be totally honest, I'm still figuring out what all of this means for me. God is still unfolding His plan and I am having a great time figuring out where this is all going. I am excited to have you join me on this journey of life, laughter, joy, and discovery.

THINK ABOUT IT, TALK ABOUT IT

Tell about a time God pulled back the curtain and gave you an exciting and unexpected glimpse of His plan and destiny for your life. What did you see and how did you feel?

How have you experienced joy and excitement in surprising ways as you walk through life?

JOY beckons us to a place of carefree laughter,
smiles, and peace in the simplest moments.

WATCH THE SESSION ONE VIDEO

Feel free to reflect, jot down your thoughts, listen, laugh, and even ask questions!

One Big Thought . . . Joy is a daily decision.

The God who made you wants you to experience delight, drink in joy, and actually have fun. He really does. This means we are partners with God in experiencing and living with joy. So, how do we engage with joy? Here are some ways we can partner with God in our journey to invite joy into our lives:

Do all things without complaining.

Change your attitude.

Replace negative thoughts with positive ones.

Focus less on ourselves and more on others.

JOY skips when others sulk; she takes risks when others cower; she works overtime looking for ways to pierce the darkness with effervescent hope.

BE HONEST

Take time to talk about any of the questions, statements, and Bible passages below, choosing what works best for your group. Have fun and be honest.

1. When you think of "Defiant Joy," what pictures, images, people, or life experiences come to your mind?

Tell a story of someone you have met who is a living example of Defiant Joy.

2. Sometimes Joy feels so far away that when she knocks on the door, we are reluctant to turn the knob and invite her in. What are some of the reasons Joy can feel like a stranger?

Why do some people push Joy away rather than embrace her?

3. The Bible tells us that God's desire is for us to have life and have it *to the full* (John 10:10). What pictures come to your mind when you think of your life being lived to the fullness of what God wants?

4. What are some practical ways we can resist and overcome the temptation to be negative, grumble, and complain? How can we invite Joy into times when there is a temptation to be negative?

Read *(together or ask a volunteer) Philippians 4:6–9 in The Message.*

[6-7]Don't fret or worry. Instead of worrying, pray. Let petitions and praises shape your worries into prayers, letting God know your concerns. Before you know it, a sense of God's wholeness, everything coming together for good, will come and settle you down. It's wonderful what happens when Christ displaces worry at the center of your life.

[8-9]Summing it all up, friends, I'd say you'll do best by filling your minds and meditating on things true, noble, reputable, authentic, compelling, gracious—the best, not the worst; the beautiful, not the ugly; things to praise, not things to curse. Put into practice what you learned from me, what you heard and saw and realized. Do that, and God, who makes everything work together, will work you into his most excellent harmonies.

5. What attitudes and ways of living are celebrated in this passage?

6. In Philippians 4:6–9, what are we told will happen when we make these shifts, and how have you experienced the truth of these promises?

7. List the eight specific things we are encouraged to think about, ponder, and meditate on in this passage:

    ✦ Whatever is _____
    ✦ Whatever is _____
    ✦ Whatever is _____
    ✦ Whatever is _____

✦ Whatever is _____

✦ Whatever is _____

✦ Whatever is _____

✦ Whatever is _____

What are real-life, practical ways we can think about keeping these things in the center of our mind?

8. How did Jesus live as our perfect example of *not* focusing on self but sacrificially serving other people? (Try to come up with some examples from His life and ministry as recorded in Matthew, Mark, Luke, and John and even Philippians 2.)

9. Tell a story about someone you know who lives a life of consistent service and care for other people. How does their lifestyle of service unleash joy?

10. What is a way you can serve someone in need as a group or as an individual? How could this become a lifestyle and not just a one-time action?

SAY yes to Joy. Jump in. She is waving at you to join the fun.

PRAY

Spend time as a group or on your own talking with God about any of the following topics:

+ Thank God for the people in your life who have been an example of self-sacrifice and humble service to others.
+ List ways to show gratitude to Jesus for His powerful and eternity-changing sacrifices for you.
+ Pray that you will notice when God is revealing your destiny, and ask for courage to follow His leading.

SIMPLE joys can carry us in a significant way.

JOY LAB
Session One

Between now and your next meeting, use any of these ideas to launch you into a life of joy, encounter with God, laughter, deep faith, and celebration.

A JOY-FILLED DAY

Try a twenty-four-hour experiment. You might even want to set a countdown timer or an alarm on your smartphone. Try to speak words of joy and encouragement all day. Commit to build people up and lift their spirits.

Do all you can to *never* open your mouth and complain, criticize, grumble, or speak a negative word. Just try it.

Pray for power and insight as you walk through this "Joy-Filled Day." Use the space provided below and on the next page to write down some notes and gather your thoughts so you can share them with your group the next time you meet:

What part of this twenty-four-hour experiment was easy for me? What wasn't as easy?

How did I feel as I came to the end of this day?

How was my day different, in a good way, because I tried to live out this challenging biblical idea?

How did this challenge to increase positive talk and refrain from negative talk bring joy to my day as well as to the day of others?

POST THE POSITIVE

Using either a separate piece of paper or the box on the next page, make a list of positive things you see or experience, things that God has done and others have done. Use the eight suggestions in Philippians 4:8 to get you thinking. Be sure to list at least ten positive things. You might want to put Philippians 4:8 as a header over your list.

MY LIST OF POSITIVE THINGS

"Whatever is true, whatever is noble, whatever is right, whatever is pure, whatever is lovely, whatever is admirable—if anything is excellent or praiseworthy—think about such things." (Philippians 4:8)

_____

_____

_____

_____

_____

_____

_____

_____

_____

Post this list where you will see it every day. It could be a screen saver on your computer, or a note on your refrigerator, bathroom mirror, above your bed, you name it. Why not post it in all these places? Each time you look at it, let your thoughts shift to positive, God-honoring things.

If you want to get really bold, post this list of positive and joy-filled things on social media where others will read it and be inspired. Use the hashtag: #MyWhateverIs to see what others are posting as well as to find your own inspiration.

SEE AND SERVE

Put some effort into being tuned in to the needs all around you. When you see a need, take action and fill it. It could be something that takes fifteen seconds, fifteen minutes, or half a day. It could be as simple as giving someone a bottle of water, a few dollars, or slowing down to speak a kind word. It might be taking a morning to join a service team from your church or helping with a community service project. Listen for the nudges and whispers of the Holy Spirit of God and respond!

Make a list of what you were led to do, who you did it for, and the impact of this action. Keep a record of at least three service actions that you took part in:

What I did: _____

How did it make me feel?

How did it impact someone in a positive way?

Joy that came from this:

How I could do this again or expand on this:

What I did: _____

How did it make me feel?

How did it impact someone in a positive way?

Joy that came from this:

How I could do this again or expand on this:

What I did: _____

How did it make me feel?

How did it impact someone in a positive way?

Joy that came from this:

How I could do this again or expand on this:

PLAY is not something that happens to you.
It's something you choose and pursue.
Look for opportunities to play.

GO PLAY

Get out and play this week and then answer the following questions:

I played today and it felt _____.

I think I felt that way because:

I want to feel more of that because:

I'm going to make that happen by:

If you had playtime with a friend, how did it feel to laugh, delight, and enjoy this time together?

JOY is fully present and content where she is: to play in the sand, breathe in the ocean air, and count the colors that cascade over the horizon while hiding that secret moment in her heart.

FOR OVERACHIEVERS AND HOMEWORK LOVERS

The Bible teaches a lot about joy. If you want to explore some of the Bible's teachings on joy and other topics from this session, consider reading the following chapters in the coming week.

✦ Day 1: Philippians 1
✦ Day 2: Philippians 2
✦ Day 3: Philippians 3
✦ Day 4: Philippians 4
✦ Day 5: James 1

Note: If you want to read more about having a positive attitude, check out the prologue and chapter 1 in *Laugh It Up!*

Session Two

KNOW HOPE, KNOW JOY

CHECKING IN

Take a few minutes to talk about what you have been experiencing this past week.

- ✦ If you tried to live a fully engaged, joy-filled day in the last week, tell about how it went for you.
- ✦ If you posted a list of positive things, how did this inspire you to keep your mind on what is beautiful, good, and worth thinking about?
- ✦ If you did a service project, how did this bring joy to you and others?

If You Wanna

By now, you know I love games, fun, and playing. So, let's play a little game as we start this session. The game is called, "If You Wanna."

All you do is read the "If you wanna" statement and make your best guess how to finish the "You gotta . . ." part of the statement. Remember, the person leading the game gets to decide on the right answer ☺.

Here's an example:

If you wanna paycheck . . . You gotta go to work.

Now you try it. There are five "FUN" points available, and potential answers are at the end of this session (no peeking).

1. If you wanna drive a car . . . You gotta _____.
2. If you wanna good friend . . . You gotta _____.
3. If you wanna laugh . . . You gotta _____.

4. If you wanna dance . . . You gotta _____.

5. If you wanna experience joy . . . You gotta _____.

THINK ABOUT IT, TALK ABOUT IT

Hint: In order to know Joy, you gotta know Hope. So, how would you define the concept of hope?

What grows hope in us?

HOPE is like a muscle—it takes practice to believe it and live it out. It takes a willful decision to hope in an unseen future.

WATCH THE SESSION TWO VIDEO

Feel free to reflect, jot down your thoughts, listen, laugh, and even ask questions!

One Big Thought . . . Hope is the anchor of joy and Jesus is the anchor of hope.

This might surprise you, but joy is not the main thing. Hope is the anchor of joy. Without hope, we will lose our joy. Once we have hope, we discover that Jesus is the anchor of true and lasting hope. If you want joy, hold on to hope. When you have true hope, you meet Jesus face to face.

Hope is the anchor of joy.

Jesus is the anchor of all lasting hope.

Put your trust in the authority of God.

God has good and amazing plans for you . . . anchor your hope to that reality.

HOPE is the reason Joy stays the course.

BE HONEST

Take time to talk about any of the questions, statements, and Bible passages below, choosing what works best for your group. Have fun and be honest.

1. How is hope an anchor for joy? When we have solid and lasting hope, how does this lead naturally to increased joy in our lives?

Read *(together or ask a volunteer) Hebrews 6:19–20a.*

> [19]We have this hope as an anchor for the soul, firm and secure. It enters the inner sanctuary behind the curtain, [20]where our forerunner, Jesus, has entered on our behalf.

2. What has Jesus done, and what is He doing today that can give us hope?

3. Tell about how Jesus has increased your hope and filled you with joy.

4. In Psalm 16:11 we are reminded that in God's presence is *fullness of joy* and *eternal pleasures*. That should blow our minds! Use your imagination and describe some of the eternal pleasures you think God has stored up for all of those who have placed their hope in Jesus and made Him their anchor.

5. If you have placed your hope in Jesus, describe how that happened for you. Tell your story of when you discovered God's love for you and how Jesus has become the one true anchor of your soul and life.

6. Hope will grow when we put our trust fully in the God who loves us. Over and over in the Bible God invites us to shift our trust from self to Him. Why is it so important that we learn to trust God and *not* rely on our own abilities and instincts?

7. Tell about one area in your life where you are really growing in your trust of God. How is this increasing your hope and joy?

8. What are some of the misconceptions that you may have of God? Why is it so important for us to know that God loves us and has good plans for each of us?

Read *(together or ask a volunteer) Jeremiah 29:11.*

"For I know the plans I have for you," declares the Lord, "plans to prosper you and not to harm you, plans to give you hope and a future."

9. Do you really believe that God has a plan for you personally?

If we really believe that God wants to offer us His good plans and a hope filled-future, how would we respond to Him and interact with Him?

10. In what practical and simple ways can we begin to place our hope more fully in Jesus on a daily basis? What is *one* action you can take in the coming week to put into practice one of these ideas?

THE secret sauce to joy is actually holding on to hope and faith
that it will most certainly get better even if it gets worse.

PRAY

Spend time as a group or on your own talking with God about any of the following topics:

✦ Ask God to increase your hope and the hope in the hearts of your group members.
✦ Thank Jesus for being the true anchor for your life.
✦ Invite God to help you notice where He is prospering you and giving you a future.
   Then, thank Him for these things.

IF I am not actively believing in hope, I cannot experience joy.

JOY LAB

Session Two

Between now and your next meeting, use any of these ideas to launch you into a life of joy, encounter with God, laughter, deep faith, and celebration.

FIRST THINGS FIRST

Commit to waiting to eat any physical food until you have consumed some spiritual food. Since Jesus is the "Living Water" and "Bread of Life," this will mean getting some time with Him. Be creative and don't lock yourself into one way of feasting on the goodness of Jesus. Here are a few ideas to get you started:

- ✦ Read a bit of the Bible (maybe the passages found at the end of each study).
- ✦ Listen to a passage of the Bible. Just use a Bible app and hit the speaker. Your phone will read the Bible to you!
- ✦ Tell God what you are thankful for and do it in the Name of Jesus.
- ✦ Write down a prayer of thanks, or confession, or need.
- ✦ Take a walk with Jesus and notice cool stuff He has made. As you walk, tell Him, "Nice job!"
- ✦ Text a prayer and verse from the Bible to a friend and let them know Jesus loves them.
- ✦ Come up with ideas of your own. Just connect with Jesus. Then, y'all, have a great breakfast! (Record your weeklong experiences on the following pages.)

WHAT I DID AND HOW IT CONNECTED ME TO JESUS

MONDAY

My spiritual food this morning:

How I felt anchored to Jesus:

How this gave me hope:

TUESDAY

My spiritual food this morning:

How I felt anchored to Jesus:

How this gave me hope:

WEDNESDAY

My spiritual food this morning:

How I felt anchored to Jesus:

How this gave me hope:

THURSDAY

My spiritual food this morning:

How I felt anchored to Jesus:

How this gave me hope:

FRIDAY

My spiritual food this morning:

How I felt anchored to Jesus:

How this gave me hope:

SATURDAY

My spiritual food this morning:

How I felt anchored to Jesus:

How this gave me hope:

SUNDAY

My spiritual food this morning:

How I felt anchored to Jesus:

How this gave me hope:

SCRIPTURE SEARCH

Take time to search the Bible for one verse that speaks about God's faithfulness and love for you. You can do a Google search, use a concordance (that's a fancy word for a book that lists every word in the Bible and all the passages that use that word), ask a Christian friend for ideas, or simply ask the Holy Spirit to direct you and flip through the Bible.

Once you find a verse that really speaks to your heart, do the following:

✦ **My verse** (write it here):

_____

_____

_____

_____

✦ **Commit it to memory**. Write it on a card, make it your wallpaper, post it on the fridge, write it on your hand, turn it into a song, do whatever it takes.

✦ Put the message of your verse **in your own words**.

_____

_____

_____

_____

✦ **Review it daily.** Once you have memorized your verse, review it often, daily. Let it sink deep into your mind and heart.

DREAM BIG

How big can you hope and how wild can you dream? Well, God can dream even bigger. Take time this week to build a list of big dreams and hopes. Use the space provided here, or make a list in a personal journal or in your notes on your phone. Try to make your hopes match the limitless God who made you:

ANY dream that makes you come alive is a
dream worth fighting for with hope.

FOR OVERACHIEVERS AND HOMEWORK LOVERS

The Bible teaches a lot about joy. If you want to explore some of the Bible's teachings on joy and other topics from this session, consider reading the following chapters in the coming week.

- ✦ Day 1: Hebrews 6
- ✦ Day 2: Romans 15
- ✦ Day 3: Psalm 16 and 37
- ✦ Day 4: Proverbs 3
- ✦ Day 5: Ephesians 3

Note: If you want to discover more about the hope that is found in Jesus, check out chapter 2 in *Laugh It Up!*

CHEAT SHEET FOR
THE IF YOU WANNA GAME

1. If you wanna drive a car . . . You gotta *get a license*.

2. If you wanna good friend . . . You gotta *be a good friend*.

3. If you wanna laugh . . . You gotta *hang out with funny people*.
   (I'll give you a point for *have a sense of humor*).

4. If you wanna dance . . . You gotta *turn on the music*.
   (I'll give you a point for *move your body*).

5. If you wanna experience joy . . . You gotta *have hope*.
   (Y'all, just look at the title of today's session . . . not too surprising).

Session Three

JOY IS A FIGHTER

CHECKING IN

Take a few minutes to talk about what you have been experiencing this past week.

✦ If you made a point of not eating any physical food before eating spiritual food, tell your group about what you learned by doing this. Did your day start better? What was some of the spiritual food that you feasted on? Did your physical food taste better when you finally ate?

✦ If you did a Bible search to find a verse about God's faithfulness, what verse did you choose, and how did it speak to you throughout the week? If you memorized the verse, feel free to share it with your group. If you turned it into a song to remember it . . . sing away!

✦ Tell your group members about one or two of the Big Dreams you have been thinking about this past week. If you have felt inspired to act on one of these dreams, tell about what you have done (or what you are doing).

Put On the Gloves

Sometimes we get the impression that anyone who follows Jesus is expected to be gentle, passive, and always kind. Smiles, hugs, rainbows, and butterflies should mark the life of anyone who follows God.

Guess what, that's not the whole story. Don't get me wrong. Christians should be the happiest people in the world. But we are also scrappers! We are fighters! There are times when the most Jesus-like thing we can do is put on our boxing gloves, get in the ring, and start slugging away.

I know, some of you are saying that every movie you've ever seen portrays Jesus as a gentle man who never got angry, intense, or upset. Here's the truth: If that is the way you see Jesus, then you were not told the whole story. Jesus put on the gloves for you and fought to set you free. He battled sin. Y'all, He delivered a knockout punch to the devil. He still fights for you and me.

When it comes to how we live our lives, Jesus calls us to fight for joy. It will not be handed to us without a battle. The good news is, in the power of Jesus, we can win. Even Joy is a fighter! So, lace up your gloves, get in the center of the ring, and listen for the bell. Then, swing away!

THINK ABOUT IT, TALK ABOUT IT

What are some of the things God wants us to fight against?

Tell about a time you put the gloves on, fought for what was right, and saw a victory.

YOU are worthy of joy, and no one can take that away from you.

WATCH THE SESSION THREE VIDEO

Feel free to reflect, jot down your thoughts, listen, laugh, and even ask questions!

One Big Thought . . . We must fight for joy, and fight to keep it.

There are enemies of Joy that seek to take it away from us. Thankfully, Joy is a fighter! We need to join in the battle and do our part to beat back the enemies of Joy. The three big foes of Joy are: Guilt, Shame, and Apathy. In partnership with God, we can defeat these enemies and walk in ever-increasing joy.

Joy is a sign of maturity, not immaturity.

God does not want you to live under the weight of **guilt**.

Jesus is ready and able to take away your **shame**.

The Spirit of God can remove **apathy** and give you fresh passion.

YOU are the one to give Joy full right to occupy every part of your present, every longing for your future, and every disgrace from your past.

BE HONEST

Take time to talk about any of the questions, statements, and Bible passages below, choosing what works best for your group. Have fun and be honest.

1. If we are going to fight and win, we must identify our opponent. What are some of the opponents Christians will face if we try to follow the ways of Jesus?

   How is joy one of the best offensive ways to fight against these opponents?

2. When it comes to joy, we are not born with a certain measure of it. It is not that some people have joy and others don't. The truth is, we all have to develop our joy and increase it by making the right daily choices. What are some specific choices we can make that will help us live with joy and grow in joy?

3. What are some of the things that can get in the way of us growing in joy, and how can we put on the gloves and fight against these?

Read *(together or ask a volunteer) James 1:2–4.*

²Consider it pure joy, my brothers and sisters, whenever you face trials of many kinds, ³because you know that the testing of your faith produces perseverance. ⁴Let perseverance finish its work so that you may be mature and complete, not lacking anything.

4. Honestly, this can seem like a very strange Bible passage when you first read it. Why would anyone consider it joy when they face times of struggle, challenge, and trials? Tell about a time you persevered, grew, and learned something very valuable when you went through a trying time.

5. Respond to this statement: *When a person faces trials with the right attitude and spirit, he or she actually ends up more mature and joyful than those who never face hard times.*

Tell about a friend you know who has faced real trials and struggles in life but has become mature and deeply joyful as a result. What have you learned from this person's example?

6. Guilt often speaks to us that our sin is what crucified Jesus on the cross. It was Christ's love that made Him give His life for us on the cross . . . NOT your guilt. How do John 10:11 and John 15:13 show this to be true?

7. Shame attacks your identity like a thief and tries to steal your joy. If you live with constant shame, this will impact the joy Jesus wants you to possess. One of the best ways to defeat shame is with a solid left hook of truth square in the jaw. We have to identify the lies about ourselves and fight back with truth. What are some of the lies that bring us shame, and what truth does God speak that will set us free from shame?

8. If we let Guilt and Shame move into our heart and stay, they will invite their best friend Apathy to join them. Apathy causes us to say things like, "I'll never change; I'll never be better; I'm not worth anything; I don't care." Worst of all, we can begin to think that God does not care about us, and then we just give up. What are some consequences we might face if we become apathetic?

    What are some of the benefits in our life (and for those around us) as we pound on apathy?

Read *(together or ask a volunteer) Hebrews 12:4–11.*

[4]In your struggle against sin, you have not yet resisted to the point of shedding your blood. [5]And have you completely forgotten this word of encouragement that addresses you as a father addresses his son? It says,

> "My son, do not make light of the Lord's discipline,
>> and do not lose heart when he rebukes you,
> [6]because the Lord disciplines the one he loves,
>> and he chastens everyone he accepts as his son."

[7]Endure hardship as discipline; God is treating you as his children. For what children are not disciplined by their father? [8]If you are not disciplined—and everyone undergoes discipline—then you are not legitimate, not true sons and daughters at all. [9]Moreover, we have all had human fathers who disciplined us and we respected them for it. How much more should we submit to the Father of spirits and live! [10]They disciplined us for a little while as they thought best; but God disciplines us for our good, in order that we may share in his holiness. [11]No discipline seems pleasant at the time, but painful. Later on, however, it produces a harvest of righteousness and peace for those who have been trained by it.

Now, **read** *(together or ask a volunteer) Hebrews 12:4–11 in The Message paraphrase.*

[4-11]In this all-out match against sin, others have suffered far worse than you, to say nothing of what Jesus went through—all that bloodshed! So don't feel sorry for yourselves. Or have you forgotten how good parents treat children, and that God regards you as *his* children?

> My dear child, don't shrug off God's discipline,
>> but don't be crushed by it either.
> It's the child he loves that he disciplines;
>> the child he embraces, he also corrects.

God is educating you; that's why you must never drop out. He's treating you as dear children. This trouble you're in isn't punishment; it's *training*, the normal experience of children. Only irresponsible parents leave children to fend for themselves. Would you prefer an irresponsible God? We respect our own parents for training and not spoiling us, so why not embrace God's training so we can truly *live*? While we were children, our parents did what *seemed* best to them. But God is doing what *is* best for us, training us to live God's holy best. At the time, discipline isn't much fun. It always feels like it's going against the grain. Later, of course, it pays off handsomely, for it's the well-trained who find themselves mature in their relationship with God.

9. God wants us to stand up, leave guilt and shame behind, and fight for the life and joy He offers. God wants to train us and grow discipline in us (like a great athlete) so that we can fight for joy. What are some of the ways God lovingly disciplines His children? How is this training good for us, and how does it give fuel for a joyful life?

10. Joy calls you to fight for the abundant life that has already been promised to you by your loving Father. In what area of your life do need to fight for joy right now, and what is one action you will take to continue to receive all God has for you?

A heart full of joy doesn't fear correction; it welcomes it, because correction offers us the opportunity to grow.

PRAY

Spend time as a group or on your own talking with God about any of the following topics:

✦ Ask Jesus to help you reject and turn away from any and all guilt and shame because He has already taken them on Himself and set you free.

✦ Invite the Holy Spirit to show you any place you have become apathetic, and pray for new commitment to follow Jesus with passion.

WHEN you exchange the familiar paths of Shame to blaze new trails toward Joy, the terrain might be rougher and it might be unknown, but you will always be trading up.

JOY LAB

Session Three

Between now and your next meeting, use any of these ideas to launch you into a life of joy, encounter with God, laughter, deep faith, and celebration.

FIVE SMALL ROCKS

Gather five small rocks or stones (from your yard, from "out in nature," or buy a small bag at a craft store). Then, use a marker to write a struggle (in one word, if possible) on each one. It could be any way you are living in guilt, shame, or apathy. Write the same five struggles on the illustration on the following page.

WHAT'S ON YOUR ROCK?

DRAW ON THE REMAINING FIVE ROCKS THE WORDS YOU CHOSE TO WRITE
ON THE ROCKS YOU'LL CARRY ALL WEEK LONG.

JOY IS A FIGHTER   61

Carry these rocks with you all week long. Be sure they are somewhere you will notice them, feel them, remember them. Then, use the space provided below to record your thoughts.

As I carried my rocks (reminders of the weight of guilt, shame, and apathy), I felt . . .

When I thought about these specific sources of guilt and shame, I realized that Jesus has already done everything that needs to be done to get rid of them. So, why am I still carrying them in my heart and life? What brings familiarity and comfort by holding on to these thoughts and ideas?

Bring these rocks to your group next week and do three things:

1. Throw them away! Throw them into the woods, throw them into a field, put them in the trash, just put them somewhere you will never see them again. (Don't throw them in the street or anywhere dangerous!)
2. Remind each other that you are free from shame, guilt, and apathy through the love and sacrifice of Jesus.
3. Lift up prayers of thanks for the freedom you have. Thank God for His love. Let Jesus know you are thankful for the price He paid to set you free. Ask for the Holy Spirit to be a reminder daily to drop the weight of guilt, shame, or apathy again.

LIGHTEN YOUR LOAD

Try an opposite homework assignment from your rock experiment. This time, take something very light (I would suggest tissues or wide rubber bands to wear on your wrist) and on each one write down a word such as: Freedom, Joy, Forgiveness, Laughter, Play, Celebration, Confidence, Grace . . . you choose.

Write these words here:

    1. _____

    2. _____

    3. _____

    4. _____

    5. _____

Carry these light reminders with you all week long. Be sure they are somewhere you will notice them, see them, remember them. Then, use the space provided below to record your thoughts.

As I carried my tissues, post-it notes, feathers, or whatever I wrote my words on, I felt . . .

When I thought about these specific words of love and God's goodness, I was reminded that Jesus has already done everything that needs to be done to get rid of my sadness and sorrow. How can I walk and live in greater joy, knowing these truths are deep in my soul?

When the week is over, put these simple reminders somewhere you will see them on occasion and be reminded of the joy that is yours through Jesus!

DON'T expect a joyful life while you entertain and host lies that seek to steal, kill, and destroy your joy.

FOR OVERACHIEVERS AND HOMEWORK LOVERS

The Bible teaches a lot about joy. If you want to explore some of the Bible's teachings on joy and other topics from this session, consider reading the following chapters in the coming week.

+ Day 1: James 1
+ Day 2: Romans 3
+ Day 3: John 10
+ Day 4: John 15
+ Day 5: Hebrews 12

Note: If you want to read some stories about being free from shame, guilt, and apathy, check out chapters 3–5 and 10 in *Laugh It Up!*

Session Four

JOY IS NOT ARROGANT, BUT SHE IS CONFIDENT

CHECKING IN

Take a few minutes to talk about what you have been experiencing this past week.

+ What is one of the words you wrote on your rocks last week? Why did you write this word?
+ What did it feel like to carry these rocks around with you all week? Did you ever feel like just throwing them away and being done with them?
+ Take time to throw these rocks away one by one. In your heart (or out loud), declare that you will not let the weight of guilt, shame, or apathy weigh you down anymore. Thank God for dealing with your past, present, and future sins.
+ Encourage each other to never pick these burdens up again, and then pray for each other, asking God to help you walk and live in freedom.

Your Identity Is Safe in Jesus!

One of the fastest growing crimes in the world today is identify theft. There are entire companies that exist to help people avoid this crime and protect them from online criminals who want to "steal" their identify. If you have ever experienced identity theft or know someone who has, it is a major pain in the backside!

Here is the amazing good news! Someone can take your credit card numbers and even compromise your finances (for a time), but they really can't take your identity. If a person has a friendship with Jesus and knows who they really are, no one can take that away: not a thief or an online crime syndicate, not you, and not even the biggest thief ever . . . the devil.

If you enter a relationship with God by putting your faith in Jesus, you are who God says you are. Your past is cleaned up! Your present is amazing! Your future is more exciting than you can imagine or dream!

Accept it. Believe it. Deal with it. You are a loved, forgiven, precious child of God—and no one can take that away.

THINK ABOUT IT, TALK ABOUT IT

Quickly list a few of the many things God says about us once we become a follower of Jesus: *"I am (and you are) . . .*

Talk about one of these new identities and what it means to you when you really think about who you are (and that no one can ever take that identity away from you).

MY identity is not based on or limited to my highlight reel.

WATCH THE SESSION FOUR VIDEO

Feel free to reflect, jot down your thoughts, listen, laugh, and even ask questions!

One Big Thought . . . Joy is most content when we know who we are.

If you accept the love and forgiveness of Jesus, you become a new person. God begins a work in you and actively partners with you to change you into the person He wants you to be (and who you really want to be). This happens because you are connected, at the core of your being, to the lifeline of Jesus. Your identity, your future, and your joy are all secure in Jesus. No one can take them away.

God makes you a totally new person.

You are a work in progress, and God is actively making you better each day.

You are connected to Jesus, the source of your life and joy.

God offers true and lasting happiness if we will stay connected to Jesus.

IN contentment I find authentic joy.

BE HONEST

Take time to talk about any of the questions, statements, and Bible passages below, choosing what works best for your group. Have fun and be honest.

1. Tell about a time you felt as if you were living backstage where most people would not notice or recognize you and what you did. How do you feel in such moments?

    Now tell about a time you ended up center stage (by choice or by accident). How did you feel when you were in this situation?

2. Why is comparison with others so damaging to our joy? What are some specific ways we can learn to appreciate who we are and where we are rather than focusing on what others have and where they are?

3. When a person begins a relationship with Jesus, they become a whole new person. The Bible says we become a "new creature" (2 Corinthians 5:17). If you are a follower of Jesus, tell about one thing that dramatically changed since you became a Christian. If you are not yet a Christian, what is one change you would like to see God do in you if you decided to follow Jesus?

4. Our growth in Jesus is a partnership. It is not just me, but God is working in me (Philippians 1:6). What is our part in our growth as we become more like Jesus? Try to come up with at least four or five examples.

    ◆ _____

    ◆ _____

    ◆ _____

    ◆ _____

    ◆ _____

5. What is God's part in you becoming more mature and moving forward on your spiritual journey?

How are you and God partners in your personal spiritual growth? How do you work together?

Read *(together or ask a volunteer) John 15:4–8.*

⁴"Remain in me, as I also remain in you. No branch can bear fruit by itself; it must remain in the vine. Neither can you bear fruit unless you remain in me.

⁵I am the vine; you are the branches. If you remain in me and I in you, you will bear much fruit; apart from me you can do nothing. ⁶If you do not remain in me, you are like a branch that is thrown away and withers; such branches are picked up, thrown into the fire and burned. ⁷If you remain in me and my words remain in you, ask whatever you wish, and it will be done for you. ⁸This is to my Father's glory, that you bear much fruit, showing yourselves to be my disciples."

6. Develop this analogy of a vine and a branch. What happens to the branch when it stays closely connected to the vine? What happens when it is cut off from the vine? What are some examples of ways we get cut off from staying close to Jesus if we are not careful?

7. This idea of "remaining" or "abiding" is very intimate and intense. It is about being as close as a mother and the baby in her womb . . . that's as close as you can get, humanly speaking. What are some ways we can "abide" or stay super close to God (try to come up with at least five)?

- ✦ _____
- ✦ _____
- ✦ _____
- ✦ _____
- ✦ _____

What is a practical way you could abide closer to God in the coming weeks?

8. Consider two or three situations in the course of a normal day in your life that can disconnect you from feeling close with Jesus. Talk as a group about how you might use those times to actually connect more closely with Jesus if you see such situations with fresh eyes and a new outlook.

Read *(together or ask a volunteer) John 15:9–12.*

> [9]"As the Father has loved me, so have I loved you. Now remain in my love. [10]If you keep my commands, you will remain in my love, just as I have kept my Father's commands and remain in his love. [11]I have told you this so that my joy may be in you and that your joy may be complete. [12]My command is this: Love each other as I have loved you."

9. Jesus wants you and me to have complete and absolute joy. He wants our happiness to be so massive that we feel it and everyone else sees it. Describe what you think a person who lives with that kind of enduring joy and happiness is like.

10. What are ways you can be an example of complete joy in *one* of the following settings in the coming week: with family, friends, at church, at work, in a social setting?

JOY knows that the secret of being content is found in being fully satisfied with who you are when no one is looking, no matter what role you are living.

PRAY

Spend time as a group or on your own talking with God about any of the following topics:

+ Ask God to help you be secure in your identity every day, whether you are center stage or backstage.
+ Thank God that you are a new creation and wonderful in His sight.
+ Thank God that no one can take away or change your identity; it is secure in Him.
+ Pray for power to abide in Jesus and stay radically close to Him at all times and in all places, through every experience of your week.

JOY looks toward the days ahead in gleeful expectation for the best.

JOY LAB

Session Four

Between now and your next meeting, use any of these ideas to launch you into a life of joy, encounter with God, laughter, deep faith, and celebration.

LIES AND THE TRUTH

Use a journal, a piece of paper, a document in your computer, or the space provided on the next page of this study guide. On the left side of the page write, "The Lies I Tell Myself," and on the right side write, "What God Says About Me." Then, list the lies as well as God's truth that counters each lie.

God will speak to you and His Holy Spirit will help you with this exercise. You might want to ask Christian friends for great Bible passages that combat the lies you are facing. You can search through your Bible. You can even do a Google search or post the lie on social media and ask others to share truth from the Bible with you. Write these thoughts and the Bible passages on the right side of the page.

The Lies I Tell Myself: *What God Says About Me:*

What have you learned about how God's truth combats lies and crushes them?

COMBATTING NEGATIVE OR LIMITING THOUGHTS

Take time throughout the coming week to make a list of any negative or limiting thoughts that wander through your mind.

Use the "Mason jar" on the next page to collect these and honestly look at them.

Pray about each of these and invite God to speak His truth to you in a way that will overcome the negative with His powerful truth and love.

THERE IS POWER IN A NAME

Go to the website: www.mykairos.org/docs/kt/names_meanings.pdf

   Look up your name. Then, write down the meaning, or meanings, of your name in the space provided below.

My name means: _____

_____

How does the meaning of your name fit who you believe you are?

How does it fit who you believe God wants you to be?

Finally, write down the meaning of your name on a post-it, on a mirror, or even on your arm so you will see it. If someone asks you why you have your name written in this place, tell them about the meaning of your name and who you know you are through the love and grace of Jesus. Throughout the week, thank God for your name and for how it affirms the identity He has given you.

ARTS AND CRAFTS TIME

Use a separate piece of paper, at least 8½ x 11 inches, preferably larger, to draw an outline of your hand.

Now, using bright colored markers, line the page with alternating colors. Start on the left edge of the page with a straight horizontal line to where your hand is and make little arches on top of the hand shape itself. Then, draw a straight horizontal line again to the edge of the right side of the paper. (See step-by-step examples at right.)

Before you know it, as you keep making lines in alternating colors your hand will look like a three-dimensional drawing.

Post your drawing somewhere that you will see it and let it be a reminder that God sees you as beautiful, colorful, vibrant, and attractive! And bring it with you to session five.

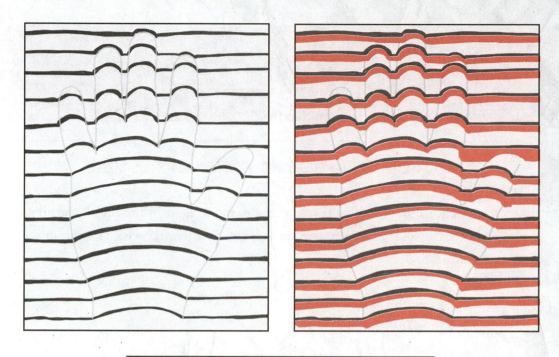

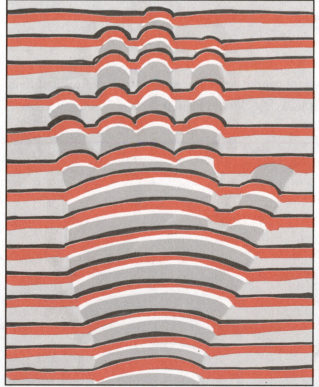

BE a full-on rebel and prove your lying list wrong! Tackle as many as you can one by one . . . every single day. When it gets tough, don't be surprised. It means you're close to a breakthrough. Keep at it and don't give up!

FOR OVERACHIEVERS AND HOMEWORK LOVERS

The Bible teaches a lot about joy. If you want to explore some of the Bible's teachings on joy and other topics from this session, consider reading the following chapters in the coming week.

- ✦ Day 1: 2 Corinthians 5
- ✦ Day 2: Ephesians 2
- ✦ Day 3: Psalm 98
- ✦ Day 4: John 3
- ✦ Day 5: Isaiah 35

Note: If you want to read some stories and learn more about living with confidence in your identity in Jesus, check out chapters 6–8 of Candace's book, *Laugh It Up!*

Session Five

JOY EMBRACES SORROW

CHECKING IN

Take a few minutes to talk about what you have been experiencing this past week.

✦ Throughout the past week, you made a list of lies you tell yourself and the truth God wants you to believe and embrace instead. Share one of the lies you hear in your heart (on occasion), and tell your group the truth God has been speaking to you that exposes and crushes this lie.

✦ Share what you learned about your name. How does the meaning of your name inspire you? Share how the meaning of your name seems to line up with who you are or who you are becoming in Jesus.

✦ If you remembered to bring it, show the drawing you made of your hand. How did this drawing inspire you or bring you joy in this past week?

Laughter and Tears

The whole family gathered to remember Papa. That's what everyone called him for the last twenty years of his ninety-three years of life. He had loved Jesus with passion. He was quick to smile, had a big laugh, hugged everyone, and poured out joy everywhere he went. Papa had loved the people in his life with deep kindness . . . family members, friends, and even strangers were all embraced with equal grace.

Before the memorial service and at the refreshment time after the service, there were quiet conversations bathed in sweet tears. There were also outbursts of laughter as stories were told and hilarious memories recounted. Many people had smiles on their faces and were laughing while tears rolled down their cheeks.

You see, sorrow and joy are not opposites. In many of life's situations, they coexist in our hearts and souls. As a matter of fact, if you look back on your life thus far, you just might discover that when Sorrow comes, Joy is not far behind. She shows up to comfort, care, wipe tears away, and whisper words of hope!

THINK ABOUT IT, TALK ABOUT IT

Tell about a time when you faced struggle, sorrow, or heartache, but Joy snuck up on you and arrived without being announced.

Why is it so important for us to recognize and embrace Joy, even in the times of life when we are feeling and facing sorrow?

JOY allows us to live in every emotion life has to offer.

WATCH THE SESSION FIVE VIDEO

Feel free to reflect, jot down your thoughts, listen, laugh, and even ask questions!

One Big Thought . . . Our emotions do not control our level of joy.

If emotions controlled Joy, then any time we were feeling down, discouraged, sorrow-ful, angry, disappointed, or a bunch of other emotions, Joy would be unwelcome and impossible. The truth is, in the toughest times of life, Joy shows up.

Joy wants to be your friend, even in the dark and hard times of life.

The story of Job . . . learning from his example:

Job's loss and pain

Job's friends (the good and the bad)

God's words and work

God is sovereign.

Joy in the morning and joy in the mourning

ABUNDANT life means we may laugh more, yes. But it also means we may cry more and feel more deeply than we ever imagined possible.

BE HONEST

Take time to talk about any of the questions, statements, and Bible passages below, choosing what works best for your group. Have fun and be honest.

1. Jesus was crystal clear that He came to give us abundant life (John 10:10). What would your life be like if you *only* experienced joy when things were going your way, pain was far away, and the sun was shining?

   How will the potential for joy increase if we experience deep and real joy even in the hard times, when pain is close, and when the blue sky is hidden by storm clouds?

2. If we let our *emotions* define our joy, much of life would be joyless. If we let *Jesus* be the center of our joy, we can be joyful at all times. How is Jesus with us in the fun, easy, positive times of life? How is Jesus with us in the hard, painful, difficult times?

    If Jesus is with us at all times (and He is!), how can this change our joy quotient in the flow of a normal day?

3. When Job went through incredible loss and suffering, his friends came and spent a whole week sitting with him and saying nothing. What message did Job's friends send to him with their presence, care, and silence? What are ways that we can be with people in times of need without trying to solve their problems or explain what we think God is doing?

4. When Job's friends started talking, things got bad fast. They tried to accuse Job and defend God. Why is it dangerous to try to explain why people are suffering (especially when they are right in the middle of it)?

What are some helpful and humble ways to bring joy and care to hurting friends and family members?

5. Elihu, the youngest of Job's friends, spoke words of compassion and hope in the midst of Job's suffering. He was not perfect, but he did speak with wisdom and kindness. What things might we say to a person who is walking through suffering that will bring the hope and joy of God?

    If you have someone close to your group, or a person in your church who is going through a hard time, what is a way you could bring joy to them in the coming week?

6. In Psalm 115:3 we are reminded that God is sovereign over all the world: "Our God is in heaven; he does whatever pleases him." What comes to your mind when you think of God reigning over us and everything in the world? How can this bring comfort and joy, even in times of suffering?

7. At the end of his story, Job looked back and saw how God had brought him through financial crisis, family tragedy, marital struggles, satanic attack, and false accusations against his character. When you look back at your life, what has God brought you through and how has He restored your joy?

In what area of struggle and pain are you still waiting for restoration, and how can your group members pray for you and support you as you walk through this challenging season?

Read *(together or ask a volunteer) Psalm 30:8–12 from The Message paraphrase.*

8–10I called out to you, GOD;
    I laid my case before you:
"Can you sell me for a profit when I'm dead?
    auction me off at a cemetery yard sale?
When I'm 'dust to dust' my songs
    and stories of you won't sell.
So listen! and be kind!
    Help me out of this!"

11–12You did it: you changed wild lament
    into whirling dance;
You ripped off my black mourning band
    and decked me with wildflowers.
I'm about to burst with song;
    I can't keep quiet about you.
GOD, my God,
    I can't thank you enough.

8. Take a few minutes on your own and write down responses to the three questions below:

✦ When you feel deep joy, what are a few of the *songs* you like to listen to or sing?

✦ When you move out of hard times and feel a fresh new experience of God's love, what are a few of the things you would *love to tell others* about your faithful and loving God?

✦ When joy shows up in the middle of the struggles of life, what specific *declarations of thanks* do you naturally lift up to God?

Share one of your songs, one of your declarations about God's love, and one of your thanks to God that you wrote above.

9. Lee Liebman wrote these profound words: "The deeper the sorrow carves into your being, the more joy you can contain." What do you think this means? If you agree with this statement, how have you experienced it in your own life?

10. In the book of Philippians, the apostle Paul wrote these shocking words, "I want to know Christ—yes, to know the power of his resurrection and participation in his suffering, becoming like him in his death, and so, somehow, attaining to the resurrection of the dead" (3:10–11). Take a few moments to write down two or three ways the suffering and death of Jesus have brought true and lasting joy to your life and to our world.

Share *one* of these with your group, explaining how Jesus is the source of joy in your life.

JOY is here for you with comfort even in your sorrow,
and with hope to help you up again when you're ready.

PRAY

Spend time as a group or on your own talking with God about any of the following topics:

- ✦ Thank God that your joy does not ride on the roller coaster of your emotions but is based on the solid rock of Jesus Christ.
- ✦ Invite the Holy Spirit to fill the deep crevices in your soul that have been formed by past pain and suffering with fresh new hope and joy.
- ✦ Ask God to give you wisdom as you seek to walk with, sit with, and care for friends who are going through hard times in life.

TRUST that God doesn't leave a single request unanswered. Whether the answer is yes, no, or wait, I choose to trust that God is innately good.

JOY LAB
Session Five

Between now and your next meeting, use any of these ideas to launch you into a life of joy, encounter with God, laughter, deep faith, and celebration.

A LETTER TO ME

Think back through your life thus far and identify a time when you faced profound suffering. Though it might be painful, remember as deeply as you can the events and feelings from that period.

Now, write a letter to yourself as if you were in the middle of that experience. What would you say to yourself if you could go back? What words of compassion and empathy would you choose? Write with love and tenderness.

When you're finished, put the letter in an envelope, seal it, and tuck it away where you will not lose it.

The day before your next meeting with your small group, take that letter out and read it. Feel the love and care you needed at that time. Drink in the grace of Jesus. Experience the healing power of God's Holy Spirit. Let the tears flow freely . . . tears of both sorrow and joy mingled together.

Then, tear up the letter as a sign that your past hurt is gone and a new day of grace and joy has come. Thank God for His sovereign presence and power in your life.

Be ready to tell your group members about how it felt to leave your past hurt behind and walk into a joy-filled future. Jot some of these thoughts below as you prepare to meet with your group.

GET TO KNOW JOB

During the coming week, do your best to read through the book of Job. It will mean reading about six chapters a day, but I know you can do it! Write a few notes about what you learn about each of the following:

What I learn about **God**:

What I learn about **Suffering**:

What I learn about **Joy**:

PICTURE YOURSELF

Find a picture of yourself that captures a moment in your past that was joy-filled, playful, and free from thoughts of sorrow or tragedy. Make this picture a screen saver on your phone, tablet, or computer, or just put it somewhere you can look at it regularly for the coming week.

Write the caption,

"Remember her? Yeah, she's still there. Let's go get her!"

or

"Remember him? Yeah, he's still there. Let's go get him!"

Look at this picture often and reflect on who you were before the sufferings of life came knocking on your door. Pray for God to help you recapture the spirit and joy of that boy or girl!

THE moments we honestly accept our loss and heartache are just the right moments for Joy to step in with hope and comfort.

FOR OVERACHIEVERS AND HOMEWORK LOVERS

The Bible teaches a lot about joy. If you want to explore some of the Bible's teachings on joy and other topics from this session, consider reading the following chapters in the coming week.

- Day 1: Job 1–6
- Day 2: Job 7–12
- Day 3: Job 13–18
- Day 4: Job 19–24
- Day 5: Job 25–30
- Day 6: Job 31–36
- Day 7: Job 37–42

Note: If you want to read some stories of how joy can embrace sorrow, check out chapter 9 of Candace's book, *Laugh It Up!*

Session Six

YOU'RE FULL OF IT

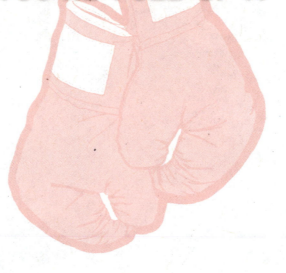

CHECKING IN

Take a few minutes to talk about what you have been experiencing this past week.

+ This past week you wrote an honest and compassionate letter to yourself. You reflected on what you would say to yourself if you could have spoken into your life in a past season of pain and suffering. What did you feel when you opened and read this letter later in the week? How is God teaching you about how joy can heal past sorrow?

+ If you took time to read the book of Job, what did you learn about God? What did you learn about how to experience joy in hard times? What did you learn about yourself?

+ This past week you looked at a picture of yourself from your past. This image captured a time of childlike, carefree joy and play. Tell about how you are starting to see that joyful spirit return. If you have the picture with you, and feel comfortable sharing, show it to the group.

Graduation Day

We have all been to a graduation ceremony. It's always a big day! The graduates sit in rows, proudly wearing a robe and a goofy hat. (Think about it, y'all, is there any hat invented that is more impractical and silly than a graduation cap?) Music of some sort is playing quietly in the background as the graduates stand up, follow the person in front of them, and walk across a stage.

There is always a dignitary, teacher, principal, or administrator on the stage handing out diplomas. This single sheet of paper in a decorative folder says it all. You have arrived. You finished the course of study. You have graduated!

As you walk off the stage, you move the tassel from one side of your graduation cap to the other . . . a bold sign that you are leaving an old life and season and starting something new. You walk off the stage as a new person—transformed, graduated!

Right? Well, sort of!

A graduation is not just the end of a story; it is actually the beginning of a new one. Now it's time to start a career, set a life direction, begin a whole new chapter. It is time to live life!

Well, y'all, this is graduation day. No need to wear a goofy hat, and you won't get a certificate to hang on the wall (but you can make one for yourself if you like). Today we finish our six weeks of thinking about *Defiant Joy* and learning to *Laugh It Up!* But this is not the end. It is the beginning of a whole new life for you.

THINK ABOUT IT, TALK ABOUT IT

Tell about a graduation ceremony you were in or attended that had something funny, surprising, or unique happen.

How are graduations a perfect time to launch a person into a whole new future?

What can group members do to make sure that today is not the end of your journey into joy but just the beginning of a whole new, amazing life?

LIFE will put you to the test. It can be difficult and unexpected, heartbreaking and hope-challenging. But Joy is a fighter. And so are you.

WATCH THE SESSION SIX VIDEO

Feel free to reflect, jot down your thoughts, listen, laugh, and even ask questions!

One Big Thought . . . We don't have to keep running out of joy; we can overflow with it!

Sometimes we think of joy as a limited resource that we have to keep pouring into an empty heart and life that leaks faster than we can fill it up. Well, this is just not what the Bible teaches. The truth is, we can live every day full of joy to the point that it overflows from us to those around us.

The journey we have been on . . .

Fountains and not buckets

Remember the sounds of joy, and invite them back into your life.

Faith . . . the center of joy

YOU may be living your worst day. But grab
on to hope that it isn't your last day.

BE HONEST

Take time to talk about any of the questions, statements, and Bible passages below, choosing what works best for your group. Have fun and be honest.

1. What has been one of your biggest and joy-growing moments over the past six weeks of this study together?

2. What are ways we can cheer each other on in joy and inspire one another to keep growing in joy even after our *Defiant Joy* study is over?

3. Look at the key lessons we've learned (below) and tell about one way you are going to seek to overflow with joy as you embrace that powerful biblical truth:

    ✦ Truth #1: Joy grows when I stand confident in who I am in Jesus.
    ✦ Truth #2: Hope is the anchor of my faith.
    ✦ Truth #3: I have to fight for joy.
    ✦ Truth #4: I can have joy even in times of struggle and suffering.
    ✦ Truth #5: Confidence in who God is and what God can do will grow my joy.

Read *(together or ask volunteers) the following four Bible passages.*

John 15:11: "I have told you this so that my joy may be in you and that your joy may be complete."

Psalm 16:11: You make known to me the path of life; you will fill me with joy in your presence, with eternal pleasures at your right hand.

John 17:13: "I am coming to you now, but I say these things while I am still in the world, so that they may have the full measure of my joy within them."

Romans 15:13: May the God of hope fill you with all joy and peace as you trust in him, so that you may overflow with hope by the power of the Holy Spirit.

4. Some people think of joy as something that is lacking, scarce, and fleeting. If you take these four passages seriously, what is God's desire for you and me when it comes to joy? What can help us embrace with greater passion and belief this truth that overflowing joy can and should be the normal condition of our lives?

5. Imagine your life is like a fountain that bubbles with joy. In hard times and good times joy can run freely, gush out, and overflow. If this was the nature of life and joy, what kind of life would we have? What would this say about joy?

Read *(together or ask a volunteer) Psalm 51:10–15.*

> [10]Create in me a pure heart, O God,
>   and renew a steadfast spirit within me.
> [11]Do not cast me from your presence
>   or take your Holy Spirit from me.
> [12]Restore to me the joy of your salvation
>   and grant me a willing spirit, to sustain me.
> [13]Then I will teach transgressors your ways,
>   so that sinners will turn back to you.
> [14]Deliver me from the guilt of bloodshed, O God,
>   you who are God my Savior,
>   and my tongue will sing of your righteousness.
> [15]Open my lips, Lord,
>   and my mouth will declare your praise.

6. Remember, King David wrote this psalm after he committed adultery, murder, and tried to cover it all up. Then he got caught, called out, and confronted! He was buried in guilt, shame, and disappointment. As you read this prayer of David, how do you see joy coming back into his life and hope being reborn?

As joy came back, how did his life change for the better according to this psalm?

7. Your deepest anxieties, worries, struggles, and sorrows are no secret to God. They are an open book before Him . . . and yet He still loves you and wants you to experience overflowing joy. Why is it so important for us to be aware that God knows everything about us and still offers us unending joy? How can we learn to embrace God's joy with greater passion?

8. What are some of the sounds that come to your mind when you think of joy? What are ways we can make a joyful sound? (Get creative here!)

Read *(together or ask a volunteer) 1 Peter 1:8–9.*

[8]Though you have not seen him, you love him; and even though you do not see him now, you believe in him and are filled with an inexpressible and glorious joy, [9]for you are receiving the end result of your faith, the salvation of your souls.

9. Being anchored in faith and knowing what we believe leads to deeper and more impactful joy. What are some of the things the Bible teaches that lead to growing joy?

If we don't believe these things, how can this decrease our joy?

10. In 1 John 1:4, we learn that there are things we can do to make the joy of other people complete. When we have joy, it is not just for us. If joy is a fountain, let's turn it on and share it with other people. Remember running in the sprinkler as a kid? Well, y'all, be a sprinkler of joy and let others run around you and feel God's love. What are ways you can shower and sprinkle joy as you walk through this coming week? How can your group members pray for you and cheer you on as you become a shower of joy?

PRAY

Spend time as a group or on your own talking with God about any of the following topics:

- ✦ Pray for God to make you a fountain of joy and not an empty bucket that needs to be filled up over and over.
- ✦ Pray for courage to be an ambassador of joy everywhere you go.
- ✦ Ask God to bless the ministry of the book *Laugh It Up!* and this study *Defiant Joy*.
- ✦ Thank God that He is the giver of joy.

JOY enables you to practice gratitude in the present.

JOY LAB
In the Coming Days

Use any of these ideas to launch you into a life of joy, encounter with God, laughter, deep faith, and celebration.

FACILITATE A DEFIANT JOY GROUP

The best way to learn something is to teach it. Make a list of eight to ten people who would benefit from experiencing new levels of joy, laughter, and hope.

Names:

1. _____
2. _____
3. _____
4. _____
5. _____

6. _____
7. _____
8. _____
9. _____
10. _____

Pray for each person by name and ask the Holy Spirit to open their hearts to an invitation to be part of a *Defiant Joy* group.

Make the ask. Just do it. Call each person, send an email, or write a text inviting them to join you on a six-week journey of joy that you will facilitate. Tell them about the impact this study has had on your life and assure them that they will have fun, they will learn about joy, and they will grow closer to God.

LEAD A BOOK CLUB

Consider asking a few friends to join you for a book club to discuss *Laugh It Up!* Each week you will all read one chapter and then come together and discuss three simple questions:

1. What was something you learned and how did it impact you?
2. How can you grow in joy and laugh more in the coming week?
3. How might you share joy with others?

IN the face of all and any odds, let your joy be defiant.
Live free and full in EVERY moment, and laugh it up.

LOOPING BACK

Review the previous five sessions of this study, particularly all the Joy Lab sections. Identify one homework assignment that you missed or want to do again and do it in the coming week. If you did all of the homework, then loop back and do your favorite one again.

And, if you haven't already, read the conclusion in *Laugh It Up!* It's a terrific summary of the book and a great word of encouragement as you move forward.

CLOSING THOUGHTS

You should be so excited and hopeful for the days ahead long after you leave these pages. And, remember, if you ever need a joy reminder or pick-me-up, you can return to these pages often. I always find it so helpful to look back to honor the past. I never long to stay there and camp out; far too many new adventures holding Joy's hand await me each day. But every once in a while, I find it healing to stand in the present, recall where I have come from, and how I've seen the goodness and faithfulness of God. My hope is that this *Defiant Joy* study will be a rear view of all the good the Father has done in and with your life. I pray that as you visit these pages in days to come, you will have realized many of your dreams and hopes. I pray the weight of guilt, shame, and apathy will be to you a distant memory. And, more than anything, I pray you find the Joy you're looking for. I pray you radiate a beautiful picture of defiant joy to your family and friends who surround you.

Thank you for joining me in this journey to live life to the fullest measure of hope, comfort, and joy. I'm your biggest fan rooting for you to live loudly, love boldly, and laugh it up!

Laugh It Up!

Embrace Freedom and Experience Defiant Joy

Candace Payne, Viral Sensation, Chewbacca Mom

The world knows Candace Payne as "Chewbacca Mom," the wife and mother of two from Dallas who captured the hearts of nearly 200 million people around the world with nothing but a toy Chewbacca mask, a smart phone, and infectious laughter.

Candace's viral moment of simple joy became Facebook Live's top video. But what the video doesn't show is Candace's storied journey of daunting obstacles on the way to the joy-filled life—extreme poverty, past trauma, and struggles with self-worth.

Laugh It Up! tells the rest of the story behind the woman in the mask. Like most of us, Candace has often felt overlooked, undervalued, and insignificant. But she has also discovered the secrets to unshakable joy that no circumstance can take away, and *Laugh It Up!* will help you discover and experience the same.

Join Candace to discover the gift God has given us all to experience life to the fullest. All you need to do is answer when Joy, whom Candace personifies as a friend, calls you to come and play.

- Do you feel tempted to give up on your dreams? Joy stays the course.
- Do your knees knock when thinking about the future? Joy hopes for what can be.
- Do you feel unseen and unnoticed? Joy is content whether backstage or center stage.
- Do you feel crushed under the weight of regret? Joy loves you enough to weep with you, but also enough to help you move on.

When life punches you in the gut, it can be difficult to muster a smile—much less a laugh. But with humor and power, wit and wisdom, Candace lights the way forward to a life that is free indeed.

Available in stores and online!